You CAN Start a Nonprofit

Douglas M. Clark

Integrated Mindfulness Media
ISBN:978-0999665008

Cover design: Kathryn Colvig, dba KColvigArt.com

Dedication

This book is dedicated to all those who have dared to make a difference through living a passionately generous life!

Table of Contents

Start serving now

Introduction
Why and how to use this book

Have you heard the story about a man who started to make a difference with just $5.00? It is one of the littlest known accounts of a gesture from a man that has made worldwide impact. You can read about it in Wikipedia. Here it is:

In 1947 Robert Pierce met Tena Hoelkedoer, a teacher, while on a trip to China. She introduced him to a battered and abandoned child named White Jade. Unable to care for the child herself, she asked, "What are you going to do about her?" Rev. Pierce gave the woman his last five dollars and agreed to send the same amount each month to help the woman care for the girl.

This encounter was a turning point for Robert. He began building an organization dedicated to helping the world's children, and in 1950 World Vision was born. The first child sponsorship program began three years later in response to the needs of hundreds of thousands of orphans at the end of the Korean War.

Over the next several decades their reach expanded throughout Asia, Latin America, Africa, the Middle East and Eastern Europe.

In the 1970s, they embraced a broader community development model and established an emergency relief division. They also began attempting to address the causes of poverty by focusing on community needs such as water, sanitation, education, health, leadership training and income generation.

With the start of the 21st century they began strengthening their advocacy efforts, particularly on issues related to child survival. They became more active in working with governments, businesses and other organizations in addressing issues such as child labor, children in armed conflict and the sexual exploitation of women and children.

Today World Vision, together with microfinance subsidiary – Vision Fund International - is one of the world's leading humanitarian organizations. Over 40,000 staff members (including part time and temporary staff and employees of microfinance institutions) implement programs of community development, emergency relief and promotion of justice in nearly 100 countries.

Five Dollars. Given to help one child grew into a movement that has now impacted millions of people.

Don't worry, you might not be a 'Reverend' – but then maybe it is better that you aren't. Why just leave it to the professionals? I think this world would be a better place if all of us chose to 'minister' to others.

I'm not saying that your nonprofit will become one of the largest nonprofit organizations in the world making a worldwide impact.

I am saying that you and I can make a difference today with just a little bit of money and a little bit of effort.

That is why you purchased this book. You want to live a passionately generous life. In fact, you could go so far as to say that is why you exist – that is your purpose.

Stirring deep inside of you is the realization that life is more than finding a job that will pay you six figures.

Life is more than buying the big house.
Life is more than having the fast car.
Life is more than touring every country.
All that is okay – but deep down inside you know that life is more than that.
Life is about making a difference and to make a difference one must have a posture of generosity.

Being generous is similar to developing a muscle. We start flexing it, building it up. Utilizing it throughout the day. At first there is some discomfort. It starts getting stronger. Soon it is as if it is just itching to be used. And once we start using that muscle, we start seeing how it improves our life and helps us help others. As it gets stronger, it allows us to perform tasks that we couldn't perform before.

Generosity is the same way once we start developing it. We start 'flexing it', building it up. It takes some effort, some discipline. There is some discomfort. Sometimes it is inconvenient. But as it gets stronger, we like how it feels when it gets exercised and we start looking for opportunities to use it throughout the day. As we do, that 'Generosity' muscle gets stronger and we enjoy the impact it makes on others and also on ourselves. We soon find new ways that 'Generosity' muscle can be used and love using it.

Soon it opens up new opportunities and new relationships and new experiences.
And, let me warn you, once you start 'exercising' your generosity muscle you will soon be living a passionately generous life. It will become your purpose.

And believe me, there is nothing, I mean absolutely nothing, that compares to living a passionately generous life.

And that is what this book is all about. Each chapter gives instructions on each step that you need to take in order to start a nonprofit. Take each step seriously. Don't be in a hurry to get to the next step because each step builds on the previous step and becomes the foundation for the next one.

Chapter 1

Your Doppelganger!

I'm just like you

Do you know why you purchased this book? Yes, I know, it is because you want to start a nonprofit. But I believe that the reason you purchased this book goes much deeper than that. You've purchased this book because you want to live a passionately generous life.

You saw a need and you want to meet it. You lie awake at night wanting to do something about it. You want to solve it. You want to throw everything you have at it. That is living a passionately generous life!

You know what, I am your doppelganger. Just like you, I want to live a passionately generous life. I want my life to count. I want to make a difference. When I see injustice, when I see lack, when I see need – I want to do something about it. That is why I exist. I exist to give. I exist to serve. And when I give and serve I truly come alive.

Please allow me to tell you a little about myself. I grew up in a family that was all about serving and giving. All my life they modeled generosity:

> Generosity of their energy,
> Generosity of their time,
> Generosity of their abilities, and
> Generosity of their finances.

As a result, I learned a lot about generosity.

When I was young, with the help of a nonprofit organization, my parents decided to move us (I have an older sister) to Latin America to give our lives in service to those who lived there. That is where I grew up until I graduated from High School. Every day of every week there were opportunities to be generous. From simply giving a sandwich to the hungry neighborhood kids to traveling for days to bring supplies and hope to far flung villages that had no running water or electricity.

We were living in Guatemala in 1976, when they experienced a horrendous earthquake, which killed over 25,000, injured more than 76,000, and left hundreds of thousands without homes.

Immediately, people jumped into relief efforts, getting medical aid to those had been injured, distributing food, and, rebuilding homes, schools, businesses, and churches that had been demolished.

It seemed like we never slept. Every moment was filled with aiding those who were suffering and working to get the country back on its feet. Thankfully, donations began pouring in to assist us.

Someone from the United States had donated an old box truck for us to use in our relief efforts. My father used it to deliver items throughout the country, traversing the treacherous mountain roads with heavy loads.

You will note that I said the truck was "donated." But it is more accurate to say it was "dumped on us." The usefulness of that truck had long passed. Not only was the engine barely able to propel the truck, the tires were bald, and the suspension was spent. If you hit a bump at any speed, the truck would continue bouncing on and on for hundreds of yards.

It was on one of these delivery-relief trips that my father hit a bump just as he was rounding a curve on a narrow strip of road, high in the mountains of Guatemala. The suspension could not cushion the shock, and he went careening off the road. The truck tipped over and slid.

Fortunately, this happened at one of the few places where the road had a shoulder. He did not tumble off the side of the mountain. And he lived to see another day.

But, I remember asking myself as a young boy, "what was the truck's previous owner thinking when he sent this deathtrap to us?"

That is when I learned an important lesson about generosity. I determined then to make sure that when I gave it would be something of value to me. Not something I was ready to throw away.

For a period of time, I had a weekly breakfast appointment with Jerry, a local businessman. Jerry was very well to do and also well-liked. Some might wonder if he was well liked because he was well-to-do. During our breakfasts, we would talk about the many things of mutual interest: politics, religion, economics, or generosity.

Invariably, at some point in our time together, he would casually remark about a person or persons who had asked him for money.

I would ask, "What did they want money for?" Sometimes the person had a reason for the request; other times he didn't know the reason because he hadn't even asked. Sometimes the purpose for the request was so outlandish that I had to pick up my jaw when I asked if he gave them money and he told me that he had.

He would literally give tens of thousands of dollars away each week—and often it was to people who were just playing on his lack of discernment.

Finally, one day I had had enough. I complimented him on his desire to be generous but explained to him the importance of being wise in his generosity. I suggested that we start a nonprofit, whenever anyone asked him for money, he first send them to me; they could plead their case to me, and I would take on the responsibility of making sure the need was valid. He agreed to my suggestion, and we enacted my plan. That is when I learned it is important to be discerning in my giving.

There are times we just simply forget to give. We have the best of intentions, but we have to get the kids to school, go on this business trip, buy the groceries—and before we know it, that good intention is lost in the recesses of our minds.

To live a passionately generous life one needs *accountability.*
Tell someone your plan to start a nonprofit.

Guess what? There are personal benefits to being passionately
generous. Among them:

> Generosity minimizes stress.
>> Would you like a little less stress in
>> your life? Then be generous. Really! Social
>> psychologist Liz Dunn conducted an
>> experiment where people were each given ten
>> dollars. The recipients were told that they could
>> keep all the money for themselves, or they
>> could give away as much of it as they wanted.
>> Dunn found that the more money people gave
>> away, the happier they felt. And, conversely,
>> the more money people kept for themselves, the
>> more shame they experienced.
>> The experiment further discovered that
>> the more shame people felt, the higher their
>> cortisol levels rose. Cortisol is generally
>> understood to increase when a person
>> experiences stress.
> This leads us to the second benefit of being generous:

- Generosity makes you healthier and lengthens your lifespan!

    Giving of yourself, whether it is time, money, or energy, actually improves your health. Dunn also studied a group of older couples for five years and examined the psychological issues surrounding caring and community.

    In all, the study examined over four hundred couples. What researchers found was that those couples who provided tangible forms of help to friends, relatives, and neighbors reduced their risk of dying by about one half. This, compared with couples who did not help anyone.

Generosity minimizes depression.

    The Center for Learning and Occupational Change examined widows to see if giving yielded beneficial results. Results of that study found that widows who were generous, whether with their time, money, acts, or words, were less likely to have their grief develop into depression. Instead, widows who increased their giving had lower levels of depression in general.

The same results were discovered among dialysis patients. When a patient undergoing dialysis practiced generosity, he or she had lower levels of depressive symptoms over time.

- Generosity enhances a person's sense of purpose.
    Somehow, when we are generous, we start believing in ourselves. It somehow seems to justify our existence.

So, if all this is true, what keeps us from starting a nonprofit?

I believe that all of us have an innate desire to be generous. For some, it is fully awake. For some, it lies dormant. For others, it occasionally raises its head and makes a noble attempt and then, for a number of reasons, drops below the surface again.

Why do we not act on this desire to be generous?
    Maybe it is because of a fear of failure.
    Maybe it is because of a lack of information.
    Maybe it is because of a lack of accountability.

Since helping Jerry with his desire to live a passionately generous life, it has been my privilege to help countless others start their own nonprofit. After helping them start I have then come along side of them and helped them lead and develop their organization so that it could meet the need for which it was established.

I want you to carry out that passion that burns inside of you. Maybe it is to help form a fine arts community (done that). A pet rescue (done that). Assist Cancer survivors (done that). Family fitness camps (done that). I've helped people do all those and more.

I want you to succeed. I want you to experience these incredible benefits of living a passionately generous life. I want you to live out your passion. I want your nonprofit to be successful.

A nonprofit started by a person just like you that is making a difference....

Anthem Pets

Anthem Pets, a 501 (c)(3), 100% volunteer rescue, is proudly celebrating 11 years of valued and trusted service in Anthem, Arizona. Our area of coverage within Anthem is Arroyo Grande, Arroyo Norte, Anthem Parkside, Anthem Country Club, and Tramonto south to Dove Valley.

Our goal is to implement a fully rounded animal welfare program that provides education and resources to the community and promotes responsible pet ownership. Since 2005 the organization has grown in size and strength and our passion runs deep in this community.

Volunteers work tirelessly to provide many services for animals and pet owners in Anthem. We provide medical care for abandoned and abused animals and find them qualified, loving homes. We work to reunite lost pets with their owners through use of a Pet Hotline and a very active Facebook page. Anthem Pets also collects and distributes re-bagged pet food to residents in need, and provides several low-cost vaccination and microchip clinics throughout the year.

Chapter 2
Let's do it!
Committing to Start a Nonprofit

Have you ever wanted to meet a need only to run into a number of challenges?

For example, maybe you want to give food to the hungry but need money to do it. When you ask people if they will give, most ask if they can have a receipt. Others will ask who is making sure that the money reaches its intended target. Others will ask if you have insurance in case someone gets injured in the process. Some will ask who is helping you.

I learned early that the best way to live a passionately generous life was through a nonprofit. I founded my first one when I was 21. Since then I have helped countless others establish nonprofits so that they too could live passionately generous lives.

There are many reasons why establishing a nonprofit is the best vehicle to living a passionately generous life.

Let's look at a few of them:

- Accountability.

  For some, accountability is like a bad word. Something to be avoided at all costs. When they think of accountability they think of a nagging nanny or a barking coach who is looking for a reason to reprimand. However, accountability is a very healthy way to stay motivated and to keep on track. Establishing a nonprofit provides accountability. You are accountable to your friends and family whom you shared your dream with. You are accountable to your Board who are carrying the fiduciary responsibility of making sure all aspects of the organization pass the muster of the IRS. You are accountable to your donors who gave money with the understanding that it would be used to further the cause for which your nonprofit was established. You are accountable to the IRS because each year you will have to report to them how you spent the money donated to your organization.

- Teamwork.

  In America, we idolize the Lone Ranger. We constantly celebrate rugged individualism and put it on a pedestal. There is something beautiful and necessary about that Pioneer who strikes out into the wilderness where no one has gone before. There is something honorable about that person who makes a stand and swims upstream and refuses to become part of the status quo. Both of those attributes are needed when establishing a nonprofit. However, along with that is the crucial benefit in having a team.

Yes, it may seem that often it is easier to work alone. You don't have to ask anyone if they agree with your decision. You can do things your way. However, establishing a nonprofit introduces you to the fantastic dynamic of teamwork. And through teamwork we discover that together we can accomplish so much more than we can as individuals.

- Donor 'Buy in'.
  If someone were to ask you for $10,000 and when you asked them why they needed it they said, 'Because, I want to do something good!" Would you give it to them? Probably not – see

the paragraph about discernment in the Introduction of this book. But if they asked you for $10,000 and they told you they had organized as a nonprofit organization, had been recognized as a nonprofit corporation under section 501(c)3 of the Internal Revenue Service. That they had a board of 5 individuals who had accepted the fiduciary responsibility to make sure the organization was run for the public good and that they had already committed their time and money to the effort. I think you would be a little more willing to give! Am I correct? Or, am I correct!!

- Charitable Giving Receipt for Tax Credit. While the purist type of charitable giving does not look for any type of 'payback' or 'benefit', our Government recognizes that a society in which people are living generously is an inherently better one than one that is living selfishly. As a result, they want to reward charitable giving. If you establish a 501(c)3 all who give to further its cause are 'thanked' or 'rewarded' by the government with a break in their taxes.

- Tax breaks.
  You will need to make purchases in order to accomplish much of anything. You will want to stretch every nickel. If you have established a 501(c)3 you can get a certain amount of relief from taxes when you make purchases for your organization!

So, it is easy to see the tremendous benefits of establishing nonprofit (501(c)3) organization.

I love how in America we have the mindset that we can do anything. We even have an abbreviation for it. We say, "that's a 'DIY' project". We build our own home, we sell our own home, we fix our own car, we make our own clothes, we prepare our own meals, we think we can do everything and anything by ourselves.

'Do it yourself!' is a mantra that we live – and sometimes die by. This is especially true when attempting to gain recognition as a 501(c)3. However, let's be honest, gaining acceptance by the IRS is not an easy task. The path is littered with the paperwork of those who have gone before you and tossed up their hands in frustration, throwing their paperwork into the sky for the wind to scatter the lost dream, never to be pursued again.

If I had a $100.00 for every story I have heard like this, I could almost retire!

Or, maybe we have heard that there is an Accountant down the road or a Lawyer across the way who will submit the paperwork for us. While there are many Accountants and Lawyers who would do a great job of submitting your application, it is not always the case.

In fact, a group of people just reached out to us who had great intentions. They wanted to preserve and develop a nearby edifice and use it for Fine Arts. They pictured having drama classes for the disadvantaged and productions presented by those drama students. They hired a person to submit their application and after burning through $5000.00 never did get their application even submitted to the IRS.

It is so much more than just 'submitting an application' – you want to start a movement. You want to make a difference. You want to live a passionately generous life!

That is why it is important to hire a mentor, a coach who sees the bigger picture. I love what I do. By asking key questions and taking crucial steps we increase dramatically the chances of your success in achieving 501(c)3 status. And not only success in achieving 501(c)3 status – but in being in existence for a long time because you established a healthy foundation.

We have assisted people wanting to:

- help with farming efforts in Haiti,
- educate orphans in Africa,
- rescue pets in America,
- provide water to the thirsty,
- build houses for the homeless,
- create a fine arts community
- build churches in Latin America
- provide support for cancer fighters
- and more!

This book is so much more than just filling out an application. Over and above helping you fill out the application, we will ask probing questions which will help build a strong foundation.

We will help you articulate a Purpose Statement
We will help you create a Vision Statement
We will help you create a Mission Statement
We will help you select a Name for your organization.

We will help you identify others who can help.

We will help you establish Expectations for Board members.

We will help you choose Board members.

We will help you understand and create Articles of Incorporation.

We will help you understand and create Bylaws.

We will help you incorporate.

And more!

I am confident, that together we can facilitate your dream to live a passionately generous life.

Let's do it!

A nonprofit started by a person just like you that is making a difference....

CREOLE, Inc.

CREOLE, Inc. exists to promote the flourishing of people through job creation and agriculture in northern Haiti.

CREOLE, Inc. was officially founded in 2011, one year after the devastating 2010 earthquake. Later, another Haiti outreach called Piti-Piti merged efforts with Creole, Inc.

Creole's core project is terracing. With only 2-4% of Haiti's forest remaining, erosion is major concern. Creole works with communities to support crews who strategically place terraces on mountainsides. This helps retain critical soil for growing crops. This also helps hold back dangerous mudslides when heavy rains come. In the last heavy rains, heavy equipment had to remove mounds of mud that came down the mountains and were blocking the national highway going into Cap Haitian. In the areas that had been terraced there was no mud. In the next 10 years, we would like to terrace the entire mountain ridge that extends from Cap Haitien to the Bay de l'Acul. Depending on the area and community needs some of these terraces will include water projects that will involve a water catchment system with distribution to the community.

Family Gardens is another project that Creole supports. Family gardens promote the idea of working together while providing food and income for families. Farmers from many gardens come together to work on one garden at a time, sharing the labor and a common meal. Then they move on to their neighbor's garden and do the same. Ag techs provide coaching and expertise to help optimize the planting, growing and harvest. They also see to the health of farm animals.

Creole has spent the last few years developing a process for specialty coffee with local farmers. They purchase coffee cherries from individual farmers and process it for specialty market. They have brought some of this coffee to the U.S. to coffee roasters with a great response. This year most of the coffee we process will be sold and consumed in Haiti. by 2020 we hope to produce enough coffee to fill a container (approximately 36,000lbs) of export, and see coffee become its own business.

Agronomists are also crucial to everything Creole does. Haitian trained agricultural techs run all of their projects. They have had as many as 12 full time professional agronomists working with them full time. This number changes from year to year based on the number of projects Creole is supporting.

Other projects that Creole is working on include oxen, goats, and new this year: tilapia.

Chapter 3
Why, What & How?

Defining the need, your vision
& your purpose

Why do you want to start a nonprofit?
Why is this the best option for you?

Fortunately for us, we live in a country that encourages
generosity. It is a part of our culture. As individuals, we gave
over $390 billion in 2016. That's up from $264 billion the
previous year!

Our own government encourages generosity. So much so that
it gives tax relief to those who give to nonprofit organizations.

And that is what brings us to where we are today. You want
to start a nonprofit so that you can live a passionately
generous life. And, I might add, you want it to be a solid
organization – one that people see is worth their support. In
order for that to happen you need to have a healthy
foundation.

So, let's start on that foundation.

We begin building that foundation by answering three questions, which are the first three steps in starting a nonprofit:

Why?

Answering this question defines your organization's Purpose.

What?

Answering this question will craft your organization's Vision Statement.

How?

Answering this question will establish your organization's Mission Statement.

Let me caution you, answering these three questions is crucial. Not just because the I.R.S. is going to ask them of you, but being able to answer these questions succinctly could very well be the difference between surviving as an organization, and getting people to jump on board with the efforts and their resources.

'Why?'

So, let's get going. Everything that exists has a purpose: you have identified your purpose is living a passionately generous life. Nonprofits are not any different: they must have a purpose. You have something on your mind, in your heart. There is a need you want to meet, a service you want to provide. It really needs to be more than something generic like, "People are hungry." Or, "People need me." Or, "Pets need food." Get more specific. You need to be able to answer the question:

Why should this nonprofit exist?

What need will it serve? Take a few moments and think about the "Why?" You need to get it out of your heart and onto paper. Not just because the IRS requires it, but for the success of your efforts you need to be able to articulate your purpose. This is the first step in establishing a strong foundation for the rest of your efforts and the success of your organization.

To help you get started, the following is an example of a "Why" created for a fictitious organization:

> *There are 10,000 children and adults who go hungry each night in our city and we want to create a way to get food to them.*

The second step in building a strong foundation for your nonprofit organization is answering the question:

'What?'

You have identified the need – the 'Why' for breathing life into a new organization. Now,

What are you going to do about it?

The "What" is a purpose statement in response to the need identified in your "Why." There are a couple of very important reasons why you need to articulate your "What."

First, it is one thing to identify a need, but you also need to have a plan for what you will do about it. If you don't have a plan – how are you going to meet the need?

Second, the IRS is going to ask about your purpose. Part of their consideration, in your application for recognition as a 501(c)3 Corporation under the Internal Revenue Code, will be based on whether you have a purpose that is for the public good or not.

Building upon our fictitious example from last chapter, here is an example of an unrefined "What" statement:

> *We are going to put our energy and our efforts into getting food to needy families in our city because there are over 10,000*

children and adults that go to bed hungry each night in our city.

Now, let's refine it and make it concise:

We exist to eradicate hunger from our city.

So, what will be your organization's "What?"

The third step in building a strong foundation for your organization is answering the question

'How?'

You've identified the need for your nonprofit and proclaimed that your Organization exists to combat that need. The next step is to explain how your Organization is going to solve the need.

How are you to going to do it?

This is an action statement. It means nothing to identify a need and declare that you are going to do something about it without knowing, at least in broad terms, how you are going to do it.

Broadly speaking, how do you plan to provide the service that both accomplishes our purpose (the "Why") and solves the need you identified (the "What")?

Continuing to use our fictitious organization as our model:

> Why:
>
> *There are 10,000 children and adults who go hungry each night in our city and we want to get create a way to get food to them.*

> What:
>
> *We exist to eradicate hunger from our city.*

> How:
>
> *We are going to collect excess food from area restaurants and grocery stores, along with donations from individuals, businesses and organizations. We will distribute the food to the more than 10,000 children and adults who go to bed hungry each night in our city.*

Your turn.

Take a few moments and put down on paper how you think your organization might go about solving the need that you already identified. Once you answer this question you will have just created your Mission Statement.

Later in this book we will define and elaborate the broad terminology in your "How" statement. Defining and refining these terms will help you build your Organizational Structure and Business Plan. But this is enough for now. Let's look at the next step in starting a nonprofit. It may surprise you.

A nonprofit started by a person just like you that is making a difference...

Habitat for Humanity

The idea that became Habitat for Humanity first grew from the fertile soil of Koinonia Farm, a community farm outside of Americus, Georgia, founded by farmer Clarence Jordan.

On the farm, Jordan and Habitat's eventual founders Millard and Linda Fuller developed the concept of "partnership housing." The concept centered on those in need of adequate shelter working side by side with volunteers to build decent, affordable houses. The houses would be built at no profit. New homeowners' house payments would be combined with no-interest loans provided by supporters and money earned by fundraising to create "The Fund for Humanity," which would then be used to build more homes.

Beau and Emma were the owners of the first home built by Koinonia's Partnership Housing Program. They and their five children moved into a concrete-block home with a modern kitchen, indoor bathroom and heating system, replacing the unpainted, uninsulated shack with no plumbing where they had previously lived.

In 1973, the Fullers decided to take the Fund for Humanity concept to Zaire, now the Democratic Republic of Congo. After three years of hard work to launch a successful house building program there, the Fullers then returned to the United States and called together a group of supporters to discuss the future of their dream: Habitat for Humanity International, founded in 1976.

The times have changed, the build site locations have grown in number, but the very real change that Beau and Emma's family experienced is shared by families today who partner with Habitat to build or improve a place they can call home. Thanks in no small part to the personal involvement of former U.S. President Jimmy Carter and his wife, the awareness they have raised, Habitat now works in nearly 1,400 communities across the U.S. and in approximately 70 countries and has helped 9.8 million people achieve strength, stability and independence through safe, decent and affordable shelter.

Chapter 4
What's your Name?

Choosing a Name for your Organization

"What's your name?" Growing up that is almost always the first question that we are asked and that we ask others. Names are important.

Parents labor for hours if not days and even months as they try to decide on the perfect name for their kids. Sometimes parents want to name their kids after someone, maybe a grandfather or a couple of different individuals that have impacted them. Sometimes they are just going for something that sounds good or something that symbolizes a special moment in their lives.

Often parents want their children's names to mean something. There are tons of books written that give the meaning of different names. Have you ever wondered about organizations and their names? I am fascinated by the etymology of names. Here are a few that may intrigue you.

Can you guess the names of these companies?
- The founder of this company, Ingvar

Kamprad formed this name by combining his initials, I.K. with the first letters of Elmtaryd and Agunnaryd, the farm and village where he grew up.

- The name of company is the combination of two Danish words "leg got" that mean "play well."
- Originally called "Kwanon" for a Buddhist goddess, this company changed its name to Canon in 1935 to appeal to a worldwide audience.
- The name of this company is derived from 'sonus', the latin word for sound and a slang expression "sonny boy", which in the 1950's the Japanese used to describe "smart, presentable young men."
- The name of this company was strategically chosen by its founders to sound Danish and "convey an aura of the old-world tradition and craftsmanship.

Are you having fun? Here are a few more.

- This company's name is both an acronym for "yet Another Hierarchical Officious Oracle" and an imaginary species described as rude, noisy and violent in Jonathan Swift's "Gulliver's Travels.

- This company was originally named 'Brad's drink' after inventor Caleb Bradham, It later changed its name in 1898 getting it from the word "dyspepsia", which means indigestion, mean to represent Bradham's belief that it was a healthy, digestion-aiding cola.

- This company takes its name from the mathematical term for the numeral 1 followed by 100 zeros.

- One colleague famously suggested this name by remarking, "we're complete virgins at business".

- This name was coined in 1999 because the keys on the device resembled the drupelets on the fruit.

- Cofounders Daniel Ek and Martin Lorentzon were brainstorming names when Ek misheard an idea. Embarrassed by its randomness, they now say the name stems from the words "spot" and "identify."

- This name started as the code for a project that cofounders Larry Ellison and Bob Oats worked on for the CIA. It was a database that was supposed to be able to answer any question about anything.

- This company took its name from the first mate in Herman Melville's "Moby Dick" in an effort to evoke "the romance of the high seas and the seafaring tradition of the early coffee traders".

How about three more?

- An alternative spelling of 'rhebok,' the Afrikaans-Dutch word for a type of antelope, this name is meant to evoke speed and grace.
- Whittled down from the original name of 'Sky to Peer-to-Peer".
- The owner of this name reportedly wanted a name that began with "A" so it would appear near the top of an alphabetical list. He thought the world's largest river was apt name for what he hoped could be the world's biggest business.

Here are the answers. I hope you didn't peek! IKEA, LEGO, Canon, Sony, Haagen-Dazs, Yahoo, Pepsi-Cola, Google,

Virgin, Blackberry, Spotify, Oracle, Starbucks, Reebok, Skype, Amazon.

What will you name your organization? This step is a no-brainer – people need to know how to identify you – but it can't be taken too lightly. Choosing a name is one of the most important steps in getting your nonprofit off on the right foot.

Why is this important?

As your organization begins to grow, a lot of the public's awareness will hinge on having picked a fantastic name.

An ineffective name tells customers that you are new, inexperienced and/or obsolete.

Also, an ineffective name will not communicate the purpose and mission of your organization. That means people who could benefit from your services probably won't even be aware that you exist.

When forming a possible name for your organization, you need to ask yourself the following questions.

Does the name of my nonprofit:

- Provide pertinent info about the type of service

I will provide?

- Communicate my values?
- Reflect the quality of my product or service?
- Invoke an image of an established, professional and responsible organization?

- Intrigue the public?

So, what will you name your organization?

In the previous chapters, we've already covered developing a Mission Statement and a Vision Statement. Now it will be easier to create a name that fits.

Let's take a moment and write down some names that you think either best describe what you are doing or are so intriguing they can be used to hook the public's curiosity.

Now, before you latch on to one specific name, you need to find out if it is available.

So, go ahead and identify your top three choices and then let's begin the search.

There are three areas that you will want to search:

- Corporation names in your State

- Domain names
- Trademarked names

The easiest way is to do this on the Internet.

To search the availability of Corporation names in your State, you may need to visit several different websites. Different departments handle this area, depending on the State where you reside. A good place to start is on the Corporation Commission website, the Secretary of State's website or a similar state agency that handles these items.

You can either register your name immediately, or you may choose to wait to make sure that a matching domain name is available and if someone else has trademarked that name nationally.

Next, go to a domain service such as GoDaddy and do a search for a domain name. You may get lucky and find an exact match. You may need to adapt your name a bit. Or, you may find a domain name that is different from your organization's name but that still communicates your mission.

Again, you can choose to register your domain name right now, but we encourage you to check current trademarks before registering. Experience has taught us that it is best to first find out if your desired organization name has already been trademarked before going through the process of registering the name and purchasing a domain name.

We have helped organizations that, unfortunately, did all their homework, except they forgot to check if the name had already been trademarked. Before long, they received a cease and desist letter from the Corporation who had already secured that name.

In one case, the organizations were on completely opposite ends of the United States and weren't even doing the same outreach work. Now the erring organization was forced to go back to square one. They had to find a new name and register it, acquire a new domain name and then start all over to raise public awareness.

If you want to search for an existing trademark yourself, you can go online and search the Trademark Electronic Search System database. Or you may prefer to let a trademark service assist you. There are a number of them to choose from and their fees can range anywhere from $99 and up.

Once you have chosen what you want to call your organization and have done the necessary research there are three more steps to follow before you can start using it. You must make it official.

After choosing a name, the next steps are to:

- Register it with your State
- Purchase a domain name
- Trademark your name

Although you have already done your research earlier to verify your desired name has not been taken, things very well could have changed since you last checked. For that reason, have a couple name choices picked out and ready so that you aren't delayed in registering.

How do you register?

Registering on the Internet

In the past, you would have been required to mail in your top three name choices and hope that one of them was available. But now, because of the Internet, registering with the State is much easier.

Go to your State's Corporation Commission website. Proceed to the webpage that deals with "Corporations." Sometimes this terminology confuses people. Yes, you are forming a nonprofit, but your organization is a Corporation in the eyes of your State (we will talk more about this later).

In most cases you can find a quick link or tab with the words "Name Availability" or something similar. If you can't find a quick link, you can type the words "Check name availability" in the search box found at the top of the page.

You then will be directed to a page of instructions about what is acceptable and what is not acceptable when choosing a name. Read them carefully!

Once you have complied with the requirements, you will find a box into which you type the desired Organization name and then press "Search." You will immediately know whether or not the name is available and if it is, you will have the option to reserve it for a period of time – sometimes up to 120 days.

If it is not available, you can input a second name choice and repeat the steps.

Once you find a name that is available you will be offered the opportunity to reserve the name for a fee. Each state is different. This usually costs extra because you are expediting the process. You will find on that page the steps that must be taken in order to have your name reserved.

Registering In Person

If you don't want to do this process online you will need to go in person to the Corporation Commission office of your State. Ask them for the instructions on how to reserve a name for a nonprofit corporation.

Purchasing A Domain Name

To purchase a domain name, decide on what domain services company you will use to purchase the domain name that you found during your research (see Session 2). You may get lucky and find an exact match, or you may need to adapt your name a bit to work as a domain name.

At this point you will have a few decisions to make:

- Do you want to purchase a .com, .org or a .net domain name?
- Do you want to purchase it for one year or for multiple years?
- Do you want to purchase a package that includes emails?
- Do you want to purchase a website package?

Trademarking Your Name

Lastly, you may find it desirable to trademark your name. We recognize it is an added expense and you may think that your "Little Nonprofit' in Small Town, USA isn't a bother to "Big Name'" organization in Big City, USA.

But, as mentioned in Chapter 4, we have had clients who have received a cease and desist letter from the lawyers of "Big Name" and had to start all over. Not only did they have to start over with the name selection process and its expense, they were forced to restart awareness of their organization within their community. Having said that, it is your choice.

If you decide to trademark your name, here is how to do it.

If you want to do it yourself, you can go to www.uspto.gov and search their Trademark Electronic Search System database and then follow the steps to trademark your name.

Or, you may prefer to let a trademark service assist you. Again, there are a number of services to choose from and their fees can range from $99 and up.

A nonprofit that was started by a person just like you that is making a difference....

Imani Care International

Imani began after founder and director, Alyssa Singh, spent a month volunteering in Kenya in the summer of 2011.

She immediately fell in love with the Kenyan people she interacted with, but her heart was broken at the dire state of their living conditions and the lack of healthcare resources within the slums. Upon returning to the United States, Alyssa could not shake the feeling deep within her that she had to do something.

She thought "do something" might mean returning to Kenya to volunteer as a nurse. However, Alyssa felt God calling her to do something else — something bigger than she had ever imagined.

In July 2012, Imani Care International was born, with the ultimate dream of providing all individuals living in the slum access to affordable healthcare services. As Alyssa witnessed, hope for the slums begins with restoring health.

Imani seeks to alleviate suffering and to empower individuals by supporting accessible and sustainable holistic healthcare.

Each project funded by Imani Care International is a collaborative effort based on the clinic's stated needs. Imani takes a supportive rather than leading role.

Chapter 5
FAST Launch!

Start Serving Now

A few years ago, a friend and I went to the fair. As we walked along the midway we passed an ominous looking attraction that was garnering tons of attention.

This attraction was kind of like a reverse bungee cord. They would strap you into a chair and then two metal arms would begin extending into the sky stretching a rubber band that was attached to the seat the riders were sitting in.

When it released it would suddenly launch you more than 10 stories into the air.

As you can expect, there were shrieks of sheer terror as riders were launched into the atmosphere

We instantly knew we had to go on it!

Unfortunately, it took forever as we stood in line waiting for our turn to be launched into outer space.

Probably the most unfortunate thing about starting a nonprofit is how long we have to wait before receiving acknowledgment from the IRS.

We know that we want to be launched into our passion. We want to fulfill our purpose. But we want to do it right now.

Currently it is taking the IRS anywhere from 12-24 months to accept your application and give your organization the green light to function as a full-fledged 501©3 organization.

That stinks.

Like all of us, you want to start making a difference now!

Guess what? I have good news. You can. You can be launched into your purpose right now.

I know a man who had a passion to see families get physically fit together. He wanted to provide a healthy exercise program that families could do together.

Included in the program would be flexibility, endurance, speed and agility. Along with the importance of eating healthy and hydration.

He had people ready to donate. People ready to volunteer and a place to hold his program.

He didn't want to wait two years to start his program. So, he didn't! He started right away.

How did he do that, you ask?

The IRS calls it fiscal sponsorship.

Let me explain. The Internal Revenue Service allows for a corporation that has received recognition as a 501(c)3 corporation to serve as a fiscal sponsor for other nonprofit organizations who do not have 501(c)3 status.

What does that mean?

It means that the organization with the 501(c)3 status will essentially be a 'foster parent' for the up and coming organization until it receives 501(c)3 recognition from the Internal Revenue Service.

In this relationship, the parent organization provides the 'house' so to speak in which the organization can grow up until it is ready to go out on its own.

Of course, there are rules that have to be followed and records that need to be kept. Which is good practice.

But with this program an organization can use its own name. Have its own website and literally function with almost all the rights of a 501(c)3 organization.

Think of this umbrella organization as your own back office, which will take care of interaction with the IRS. This allows you do what it is you are wanting to do. You can benefit from their 501(c)3 status and accomplish what you want with much less hassle.

Wouldn't that be great?

You could get up and running immediately fulfilling your desire to live a passionately generous life.

Your challenge is to find a 501(c)3 corporation that will, or can, fulfill this role for you.

There aren't very many corporations with a 501(c)3 status who are recognized by the IRS to be able to do this.

I've got some more good news.

We have established a 501(c)3 organizations that was set up specifically to serve this need.

Yep, you read correctly.

Its sole reason for existence is to help people lead passionately generous lives. As such this 501(c)3 has helped countless individuals and groups fulfill their passion as they pursued recognition by the IRS.

Remember the guy who wanted to see families get physically fit together? That was eight years ago.

What began as a two week a year program has grown into a multi-site year around program. He has a website. Major organizations donate to his efforts. He has literally dozens of families go through his program each year.

The crazy thing is, he loved living in the fiscal sponsorship 'house' so much that he decided he didn't want to pursue having his own 501(c)3!

However, there have been many organizations who have benefited from this program and have gone on to become full-fledged 501(c)3 organizations.

If you are interested in this Fast Launch opportunity, send an email to info@giveservelive.com and put Fiscal Sponsorship in the subject line.

There is an application process.

You will have to express:
1. Why your organization should exist.
2. What it is you want to do.
3. How you are going to do it.

But, that really shouldn't be too hard!

You already have all that figured out because that is what we covered in the first chapters of this book.

Another nonprofit started by someone just like you that is making a difference...

In Our Backyard

In Our Backyard (IOB), a 501(c)3 nonprofit, links arms across America in the fight against human trafficking through awareness, action, education, legislative advising and advocacy for survivors.

In 2006, In Our Backyard (IOB) Founder and Executive Director Nita Belles was exposed to the realities of human trafficking in America and realized that there was no option to "stand on the sidelines" of this atrocity. At the request of Oregon's U.S. Marshall over human trafficking, Belles founded the Central Oregon chapter of Oregonians Against Trafficking Humans (CO-OATH) in 2009, which has since integrated into IOB combining both local and national human trafficking efforts. IOB's flagship programs, Freedom Stickers and Convenience Stores Against Trafficking (CSAT) provide critical public awareness and lifelines of hope for victims of human trafficking.

IOB believes that awareness is the critical first step to ending human trafficking. IOB places Freedom Stickers in public restrooms across the country, providing hope and a pathway to freedom for victims of human trafficking. Its newest program, Convenience Stores Against Trafficking (CSAT) raises public awareness of the issue in communities across America. CSAT engages convenience stores as trafficking prevention centers in local communities by training employees to recognize and report human trafficking.

IOB works to eradicate human trafficking through partnerships with top law enforcement, businesses, nonprofits and government agencies. As a highlight of our anti-human trafficking efforts, IOB works to eradicate sex trafficking surrounding the Super Bowl. The operation began eight years ago and has continued in every Super Bowl host city since. This program increases awareness, supports law enforcement efforts and looks for missing children.

Chapter 6
Let's Frolic!

Getting others to help

I love that word! It sounds like fun, enjoyable, exciting, active – almost naughty (stop it!)!

Do you know what it means? A frolic is a work event that combines socializing with a practical goal. It is the word that the Amish use when they need to come together to build a barn or other building.

The Amish barn-raising symbolizes the values of community and hard work. The barn raising fulfills a practical need and also serves to tie the Amish community together, reinforcing Amish society through a very visible expression of the principle of mutual aid.

What would normally take weeks with a few individuals – and which would be impossible to do alone – is done in well in a short amount of time.

Wow, that sounds just like what you are wanting to do in establishing a nonprofit.

And that is where we are now in creating your nonprofit. We need to identify help. We need to invite people to come frolic with us!

These frolics in the Amish community require organization, supplies and labor. They typically are led by one or two master Amish 'engineers', who lay out plans for the barn and assure the materials are available. All labor is contributed for free as well.

Guess what? You are the Master Engineer to make sure that each participant fills a role that they are good at.

Remember when you created your Mission Statement back in Chapter 3 and we said we'd later elaborate on the terminology? The details of the statement were left broad and undefined. It's now time to address the "we" within that Mission Statement.

Again, referring to the fictitious organization, their Mission Statement was:

> *We are going to collect excess food from area restaurants and grocery stores, along with donations from individuals, businesses and*

organizations. We will distribute the food to the more than 10,000 children and adults who go to bed hungry each night in our city.

When you say "We" whom — exactly — do you mean? Who is going to help you? Is it you and your cat?

Do you have a name or a face that comes to mind when you said 'we'?

Maybe you have managed thus far on your own, or perhaps with the aid of one or two other people.

Can you do it by yourself?

Yes, you can – at first. Initially you will make great headway, it is easy to work by yourself. You can read this book by yourself. You can make lists by yourself. You can dream by yourself.

However soon you will need to do some 'heavy lifting' and you will find that, just like with the Amish, what would normally take weeks with a few people – and which would be impossible to do alone – is done and done well in a short amount of time.

You would do well to embrace the axiom, "You can go further together." You may be able to get things done faster working by yourself because you don't have to take others opinions in consideration. However, you won't get very far.

You don't have expertise in everything.

You may have bookkeeping experience. But do you know the law? You may know how to organize a flow chart. But do you know how to motivate people? You may have expertise in accounting. But can you raise all the money necessary to fund the Organization?

So, while it may be easier doing things by yourself- getting along with others can be a challenge- including others in your plan will enhance your chance of success.

Also, people will be hesitant to donate to an Organization whose purse strings are controlled by one person. They will tend to be suspicious, thinking that maybe you are just wanting to line your pockets with their donations.

I had a client that asked me to help them. They were in a mess. To be expeditious, one person had formed the nonprofit. Everything seemed to be going well until someone got suspicious and started a rumor that the Founder of the organization was using donations to purchase real estate in the South Pacific. We came in and did an audit and proved that was not the case. Unfortunately, the damage was done and before too long that nonprofit ceased to exist.

Why? Because a nonprofit must have the trust of the public in order to survive.

Most importantly, the Internal Revenue Service will scrutinize you a bit more if you are the only person on your Board and the only person responsible for accepting donations and making disbursements.

And adding a family member may not be the best solution. Nepotism has been the cause of more than one nonprofit misappropriating resources. I am not saying that it can't be done above board. However, from personal experience I can say that it will hinder donations. And on top of that, the Internal Revenue Service will not view that as enough of a distinction from you. For those reasons, consider including people who are not related to you by blood or marriage.

Who should you consider?

How do you identify those who might make a great addition to your efforts?

Well, first identify individuals who either already share a similar passion or whom might embrace it when presented the opportunity.

Include people who are on the same page as you. By sharing the same zeal, it exponentially creates more energy and leads to increased accomplishment.

You don't want to include people who aren't on the same page concerning the overall purpose of your Organization. There are bound to be differences of opinion when you get into the nitty-gritty of running an Organization. But you don't need people pulling the Organization off- track.

Next, you want people you can get along with. That may be someone who is already your friend – but maybe not. You might not be able to work with your friends. Let's expand our perspective and identify people who seem friendly, good natured, thoughtful, considerate and patient. Those are character traits that wear well when you are together in the trenches.

Lastly, look for people who have expertise. It can be helpful to have someone who has some legal insight, especially if they know the laws that are germane to running a nonprofit. A person who has bookkeeping or accounting expertise is helpful. Someone who has marketing experience can be a godsend. Someone who has organizational development skills can also be beneficial.

You get the point.

If you can, identify and include people who know how to do the things that you don't.

Initially most of your help will come through volunteers. You won't have the funds to pay for staff. Eventually however, that will change. We can help you with your organizational development so that you know when and how to expand.

But in the meantime, don't worry if you don't know anyone with any areas of expertise that we discussed here or that you know you will face. That won't stop you from being successful. Just be prepared to spend money in those arenas. You may eventually want to have access to a lawyer who knows nonprofit law. You may also find it helpful to have a bookkeeper and/or an accountant. You will want help with marketing. So, we encourage you to be on the lookout for those professionals.

We had a client who wanted to get water to people were homeless. He developed his 'Why', 'What' & 'How'. Then he went on to choose a fantastic name. After that he took his time and really developed his 'Who'. He developed a list of everyone who he could think of who might be able to help him. Then he began meeting with each one individually. Because he had a well developed 'Why, What & How', he was able to describe his vision in a convincing manner.

Before you know it, he had over 20 people ready who had embraced the vision and were ready to give of their time, expertise and finances to make it happen.

Take some time right now (and for the next few days), to assess the people you already know: people who are already in your life, maybe even outside your immediate sphere of influence.

Don't exclude people who are possibly once or twice removed. Don't exclude anyone. The bigger the list you can create, the better. We will get into the reasoning for this momentarily.

If they pass the criteria discussed above, put them on the list. Take a few minutes to jot a few names down.

Next, let's spend a couple of minutes and talk about why you want to write down as many names as possible on your list.

First, to be successful in your efforts you want to grow your sphere of influence and make it as big as possible, that is most easily done by reaching out to those you know, and to those whom your friends know.

Second, you will need different types of people for the success of your Organization. In the most basic sense, you will need managers and you will need workers. Those who are manager or administrative types will fit best on your Board of Directors. Worker types fit best carrying out the day-to-day tasks of your Organization.

Now, it is time to invite people to frolic with you. Take the Why, the What, the How that you have established for your nonprofit and begin scheduling coffee with each person on your list. Tell about the need that the nonprofit will fulfill (the Why). Tell them what the organization will do about it (the What). Tell them how the organization is going to go about doing it (the How). Tell them that you are working with me and that I am helping you put all this together.

After you have communicated all this, posture yourself to listen. Ask them if they have the same passion for the need that you identified. Ask them if they would like to have a role in solving that need. Ask them if they have any ideas.

If they ask specifically what you want them to do, tell them that you aren't sure yet. Right now, you are just trying to discover basic buy-in from your friends and acquaintances.

Be prepared, you will experience all kinds of responses. From blank stares, to 'No way', to 'Maybe', to 'Yes please!'

After you have met with each individual, tell him or her thank you for their time and then go home and record what you discovered. Categorizing them as to their current level of enthusiasm, their skill sets and their experience.

Warning: don't toss out the names of whoever isn't available to serve in one of those two arenas. The people who remain on the list will form your initial mailing list. You will want to start regularly communicating with them. These are the individuals you'll want to provide with updates about your Organization, your successes, challenges, hopes, dreams, etc.

Some might choose to donate money. Or they may pass your information to others whom they know, thus increasing your sphere of influence, who in turn may volunteer their time, abilities and resources to the cause. Who knows they themselves may even change their mind over time, become an active participant of your efforts.

Another nonprofit started by a person just like you that is making a difference...

Sister Schools

From the beginning, it has been about opening eyes and changing lives.

In 1988, Terry McGill traveled to East Africa and saw the incredible poverty and hardship resulting from twenty years of civil war and a ravaging AIDS epidemic in the small country of Uganda. He was forced to ask a very personal question,

"If I really am the kind of person I would like to think I am, then what should I do about this?"

Upon his return to Seattle, Terry shared his images with local school children. After seeing pictures of the conditions in Ugandan schools and orphanages, the response from local students was overwhelming. McGill returned to Uganda with school supplies and clothing donated by children in Seattle. As he distributed the supplies to the schools and orphanages in Uganda, he saw hope in the Ugandan children's eyes. When he returned home again, McGill showed photos of the Ugandan children and their new gifts to the students who donated the supplies. The children were able to see the personal impact they made in another youth's life.

Sister Schools was formed because McGill saw the incredible impact person-to-person giving had on the youth in our own schools and the hope that was delivered to youth in need on the other side of the world.

Sister Schools teaches compassion, service and social responsibility by partnering students in donor schools with children in need. Sister Schools achieves this through two complementary goals: First, providing students the life-changing and character-building experience of personal giving; and second, providing supplies, hope and inspiration to children in need.

In the years since the first trip to Uganda in 1988, Sister Schools has partnered with more than two hundred local schools and presented to thousands of students and teachers. Sister Schools has delivered more than three-quarters of a million pounds of supplies donated by U. S. school children to their counterparts in Uganda.

Today, Sister Schools continues the pursuit of opening eyes and changing lives.
Sister Schools teaches compassion, service and social responsibility by partnering students in donor schools with children in need. Sister Schools achieves this through two complementary goals: First, providing students the life-changing and character-building experience of personal giving; and second, providing supplies, hope and inspiration to children in need.

Chapter 7
Let's Plan a Party!

What does a Board do anyway?

Although we have been illustrating the starting of a nonprofit by drawing similarities with planning a party, this is where that similarity ends.

Yes, we want to have enjoyable people working with us and we want to have an enjoyable experience. However, serving as a Director on a nonprofit corporation is much more serious than planning a party.

Unfortunately, this is how many organizations communicate what serving on a Board will be like. "Come join us," they say, "it will be one big party!" Ok, maybe they don't say party. But they do say. "It will be fun!" or, "We will have a blast!".

I had a client who unfortunately did just that. He was the type that always wanted everything to be fun (I'm a lot like him!) and thought that the best way to convince people to serve on the board of his nonprofit was to tell them how much fun it would be. It didn't take long for him to experience some serious pushback as the new board members realized that the

Board meetings weren't a party and that the role of a Board member was actually huge responsibility!

Unfortunately, some of his Board resigned and this slowed the efforts of the nonprofit as they had to regroup and find those who were willing to serve with the understanding that it was more than just a party. I am happy to say that this hiccup did not derail them permanently, but it could have been avoided.

So, although it may be true that you want everyone to enjoy serving on the Board, it is so much more than just having fun or a blast.

In this chapter, we are going to talk about identifying the individuals who will serve on your Board of Directors and communicating to them what their responsibilities will be.

For the next few pages let's take some time to talk about 'Board Expectations'. In other words, what the expectations are for the person who agrees to be a Board Member of your nonprofit corporation.

Let's start by asking the question:

What should you expect from your Board members?

Knowing what you need and expect from your Board members — and communicating it to them before they agree to serve — will help you avoid a ton of headaches down the road. You don't want to have people lined up to help only to have them bail because they didn't realize how much work it was going to be and leave you stranded. And as the organizer, you don't want Board members who aren't pulling in the same direction.

If you put yourself in their shoes, it will become obvious. Nobody likes to agree to volunteer their time only to be told later, "And by the way, as a Board member you are expected to do this and this."

So, what should you expect from a Board member? Isn't it just enough that they agreed to serve? Just the fact that they are willing to sit through a Board meeting once a month is enough, isn't it?

Not really.

First and foremost, members of your Board need to know that they are legally responsible for the acts of the Organization. As a board member, they have what the IRS calls 'a fiduciary responsibility'. Do you know what that means? Here is the Business dictionary definition of fiduciary responsibility:

> A legal obligation of one party to act in the best interest of another. The obligated party is typically a **fiduciary**, that is, someone entrusted with the care of money or property. Also called **fiduciary** obligation.

In other words, the IRS will be watching to make sure that the Board member handles the money and property in a way that is in the best interest of the public trust. So, you can see why it is extremely important that each member understands this role.

In addition to this important legal aspect, there are many other ways a Board member will be key to accomplishing your vision.

Besides attending regular Board meetings and wrestling with issues involved in running a nonprofit, there is another major contribution that Board members provide: "Buy in."

This "buy in" is measured in four ways:

- Finances: You need members willing to support

the Organization financially from their own checkbook and willing to ask for money from others.

- Energy: You need members willing to get involved in the various events and outreaches that the Organization schedules. They probably can't make it to all of the events, but what is the minimum attendance you need from them?

- Influence: You need members willing to use their influence among peers to   raise awareness and get others involved.

- Team Attitude: You need members willing to support the Directors and staff in the tough calls that will arise. And they will need to function as part of a whole and not as a lone ranger.

Spend a couple minutes and write down what you think are the basic levels of "buy in"
you need from your Board members.

Here are a few questions to get you started:

- Finances: What size check should they be willing to write each year?

- Energy: How many events or outreaches should they be expected to attend, or possibly direct, each year?
- Influence: How many friends and peers should they recruit for the   Organization each year?
- Team Attitude: How often will they be expected to work as part of a team versus working on solo projects? Are they comfortable giving and receiving instructions and assignments?

Here are some additional responsibilities that Board Members need to understand that they will be expected to fulfill:

- Establishing Policy: Carefully select individuals who understand and believe in the purpose of the Organization.
- Decision Making: Board members will need to make levelheaded decisions in the best interest of the Organization and not based on their own personal interest.
- Maintaining Confidentiality: Most of the Board's decisions come after discussion of confidential information. It is crucial that you are able to select members who can be discreet and keep confidences.
- Selection of Executive(s): Eventually, Board

members will be responsible for selecting the Chief Executive (usually called the Executive Director).

- Goal Planning: Chosen members will participate in an overall planning process and assist in implementing and monitoring the plan's goals.

- Managing Programs and Services: Members will be responsible for monitoring and strengthening programs and services. They will need to determine which programs are consistent with the Organization's mission and determine each program's effectiveness in meeting Organizational goals.

- Raising Funds: This may come as a surprise, but outside of providing leadership the board's main responsibility is to raise funds to ensure the organization's sustainability.

It is a good practice to put your expectations in writing. Then print out copies and have your Board members sign the document stating that they have read and understood their commitment.

Once you have decided what you will expect from a Board member you are now ready to begin selecting who you would like to invite to be on your Board. Now that you are aware of what a Board member will be responsible for, you can easily see it is crucial that you take your time selecting potential Board members.

It is helpful, but not necessary, if you are able to find members who have expertise in business, law, bookkeeping, accounting and/or expertise in the realm in which your Organization is going to function.

Most of all you want members that are passionate about and supportive of the purpose for which the Organization exists.

It would be a good exercise for you right now to stop and write down 12–15 names of people who you think would be good candidates for the Board. Beside each name write down the reasons why you think they'd be a good fit. You won't need 12-15 Board members, but not everyone will say yes. Whoever is not chosen now, may be called upon in the future as you rotate in new Board members.

Another nonprofit started by a person just like you that is making a difference...

Wildlife for Tomorrow

Wildlife for Tomorrow was created in 1990 to enhance the management, protection and enjoyment of Arizona's fish and wildlife resources. The Foundation is an independent 501(c)(3) nonprofit organization that works closely with the Arizona Game and Fish Department to provide additional support for projects and education activities where traditional resources are not adequate. Wildlife for Tomorrow's efforts focus entirely on worthy projects within Arizona and no funds are passed on to national offices or to projects in other parts of the country. The Foundation does not participate in or attempt to influence regulatory, management or legislative decisions, nor does it take a position on controversial or value-sensitive issues. Its single purpose is to support important and worthy projects that make a difference to the wildlife and people of Arizona.

Through the Foundation, individuals, businesses and organizations can participate in projects to benefit all of Arizona's fish and wildlife and the habitats upon which they depend. These projects include habitat improvement, youth and adult education, research and wildlife protection activities. Please contact us about how you can help.

Chapter 8

Rules to Party By

Articles of Incorporation & Bylaws

Earlier in this book we used the metaphor of planning a party to help describe what to do when putting your nonprofit together. We decided that we were going to have a party – we called it a 'frolic'. And, in that chapter, we basically started deciding who we were going to invite to our party.

Let's run with that metaphor a little bit more. Remember growing up and your parents agreed – sometimes to their chagrin – to let you and your friends have a party?

They wanted to know:

> Why you want to have a party?
> What was going to happen at the party?
> How you were going to make it happen?
> Who was going to help you have this party?

Along with:

> Where did they live?

How could they contact them (or their parents) if they needed to?

As we plan this party, the IRS (think parent) wants to know the same thing.

- They want to know why you are going to have a party.
- They want to know what is going to happen at this party.
- They want to know how it is going to happen.

We have established all of that.

Now:

- They want to know who is helping you throw this party.
- They also want to make sure that all those who are a part of making this party happen agree to adhere to the rules that have been established for these types of parties.

And,

- They want to know how you are going to behave when you are given options inside of the laws.

In legal terms, the document that declares these things is called Articles of Incorporation. Don't let the unfamiliar wording trip you up. Think of Articles as being 'Statements' or 'Declarations'.

Also, this is where many get confused. Incorporation? I thought we were starting a nonprofit organization. Yes, you are but in order to receive recognition as a 501(c)3 you need to Incorporate. And in order to Incorporate you need to have Articles of Incorporation. However, you are going to be applying to be a nonprofit corporation.

The creating (or 'drafting') of your 'Articles of Incorporation' is the first legal act that you will do. This is your legal incorporation document. Sometimes they are called a Certification of Formation or Charter.

So, let's break down 'Articles Of Incorporation'.

The Articles of Incorporation contain general information about the Corporation. Articles of Incorporation basically tell the world and the government -
> 1) that you are going to adhere to all legal requirements, and

2) how your organization will function when the law allows you choices.

Articles of Incorporation are a set of formal documents filed with a government body to legally document the creation of a corporation (think: 'We are going to have a party!' announcement).

The Articles will establish the Purpose of the Corporation (think 'Why are we having a party!)

These Articles must contain pertinent information such as the firm's name, street address, and who is going to be the agent for service of process (think who is putting it on and where they can be found).

They will also establish:

- How many members will be on the Board and who the initial first ones will be until you have your first annual meeting.
- How you will dispense with any assets when you decide to cease to exist as a corporation.
- Limit the liability of Board members.
- That you will not discriminate.
- Lastly, whether you will have members or not.

The Articles of Incorporation are also referred to as the "corporate charter," "articles of association" or "certificate of incorporation."

Once they are drafted they will need to be filed with the appropriate department in your State. Usually, that is the office of the Secretary of State but sometimes it is the office of the State Attorney General. And you will need to pay the State a fee to Incorporate.

Although the IRS requires specific things and you should definitely have some processes and protocols laid out in your paperwork, the best rule of thumb is to keep these processes and protocols broad and general.

There are a few different reasons for this:

- You don't know what the future holds so don't try to address everything right now.
- You are legally bound by what is written within the Articles and if you fail to follow them, you are risking legal repercussions.
- Articles are foundational. They can be changed but it is very difficult.

The next step that we need to walk through is called:

'Drafting Bylaws'

While Articles of Incorporation, provide general information about your nonprofit Corporation that the State and governing authorities require. Bylaws contain information about the rules and regulations that govern your Corporation. They also help to establish the roles and duties of your Organizations Directors and Officers.

At some point, a Board Member will raise his hand in a meeting and ask, "Can we do this?" That's when your organization's bylaws come to the rescue. Hopefully, you will have them handy.

What Are Nonprofit Bylaws?

Let's go back to our illustration of when you wanted to have a party. Your parents – or whatever adults were responsible for you - were quick to establish some rules and some boundaries that needed to be adhered to if you were going to have that party. You agreed to those rules and knew that if at any time during that party you did not follow those rules your party could be shut down.

The same is true with running a nonprofit. The IRS (think parent/adult) has agreed to let you have a party. They have even agreed to give you some help in throwing the party (think charitable giving recognition and tax breaks). But in turn they say here are some rules that you have to abide by. As bad of a rap that they often get – at this point even they allow us to establish many of the rules that we are going to abide by.

Those rules are written out and we agree to abide by them and the IRS agrees to monitor us and if we don't abide by our own rules (along with some rules that they have established) – our party may be shut down.

The rules that we establish are called Bylaws.

Your nonprofit's bylaws are both a legal document and a roadmap for your organization's actions.

A required element when forming a corporation, bylaws are a form of agreement or contract between the corporation and its owners to conduct itself in a certain way. The IRS will look for your Bylaws when granting tax exemption.

While for a commercial business the owners are its shareholders, the ownership of a nonprofit corporation belongs to the public as represented by the nonprofit organization's governing body, usually a **Board of Directors.**

What the Bylaws contain varies according to the nature of your organization but consider them to be your internal manual for how you will operate.

They should address basic activities, such as:

- Governance, whether the organization is controlled by a board or by its membership
- When and how board meetings will be held and conducted
- How board directors and officers will be appointed or elected
- Voting procedures, such as what constitutes a quorum so that your board can make a decision
- How committees are created and discontinued
- The number of **directors for your board,** their required qualifications, and their terms of service
- Language that affirms the requirements and prohibitions for nonprofit 501(c)3 organizations that the IRS has established.
- Rules that govern **conflicts of interest**
- How the bylaws can be changed or amended

You can make changes to your Bylaws and in fact your Bylaws will establish how those changes can happen. Just make sure that you report any changes you make to the IRS.

An organization that is exempt from federal income tax, as described in Internal Revenue Code 501(c)(3), is required to report changes to its bylaws and other governing documents annually to the IRS on the organization's IRS Form 990.

Substantial changes to a tax-exempt organization's character, purposes, or methods of operation should be reported to the IRS as soon as possible because such changes, if inconsistent with the organization's tax exemption, could affect the organization's tax-exempt status.

For minor changes, just report them on your organization's next annual Form 990.

Check with the state where you are incorporated for its regulations for reporting changes to your bylaws

Although bylaws are not public documents, it would be wise to keep them available for public viewing. Doing so will help with your organization's transparency.

Bylaws should be used, changed when needed, and examined often. Don't let them gather dust on a shelf somewhere. Make them a working document in every sense.

However, remember that simplicity is generally the best approach because it allows you more latitude as an organization.

It is important that you intimately know and closely follow your Organization's Articles and Bylaws because these operate as your rule book. If you do something that is contrary to what is established in your Articles and your Bylaws it can open your Organization to lawsuits - think 'Your party can be shut down!'

Another nonprofit started by someone just like you that is making a difference…

BloodSource

Since our founding in 1948, BloodSource has been collecting blood donations and providing lifesaving blood products to our communities and beyond. We are committed to doing what's right, a simple philosophy that has helped us grow from a single blood bank beneath a water tower in Sacramento to one of the premier blood centers in the world.

Thanks to the generosity of donors throughout Northern and Central California, we are the source of nearly every drop of blood used in over 40 hospitals in the region. BloodSource donors from Merced to the Oregon border, from Solano County east to Lake Tahoe, are a lifesaving source close to home and across the nation to the help other blood centers unable to go it alone.

After more than 60 years, thousands of donors have given the precious gift of blood, and countless volunteers give their time and talent, assuring us all of a plentiful blood supply. In that time, our community-based, not-for-profit regional blood center has never lost sight of its essential mission: to provide blood and services to those in need.

We are committed to collecting, testing, processing and delivering blood and blood components – wherever and whenever the need.

Our ability to do so rests with our donors.

Yes, you do save lives.

Chapter 9
Nitty Gritty

Incorporating, Publicizing, EIN & More

In this chapter, we are going to deal with what I call the 'Nitty Gritty' of applying for recognition by the IRS as a nonprofit corporation under section 501(C)3 of the Internal Revenue Service.

The next step is you will need to establish your Organization's intentions in the State in which your Organization is based. This is called:

'Incorporating'

This usually trips people up because they don't realize that in order to receive 501(c)3 recognition your organization has to incorporate. Don't let that confuse you. Each State's requirements for incorporating are slightly different, but every State requires a completed Articles of Incorporation and Bylaws, which you created in Chapter 7.

Depending on the State, you will need to combine the Articles of Incorporation and Bylaws with a cover sheet containing specific instructions that your host State requires.

Take both of these items to either the Corporation Commission of your State or, in some instances the Secretary of State's Office.

Be prepared to pay a filing fee that is somewhere between $25 to $50. Remember to keep your receipt; you can be reimbursed for this expense by your Organization once it is up and running.

The next step is:

'Publicizing the Corporation'

What this means is letting the public know, in a formal way, that your Organization is now a Corporation.

Each State has different legal requirements as to how to publicize the incorporation of your Organization. Even though the requirements may be different, publicizing is a legal requirement for every Corporation.

When your State has accepted your application for recognition as a Corporation, they will send specific instructions to the Registered Agent listed in your Charter as to how to publish in your State.

It most likely will entail publishing your Articles of Incorporation in a periodical for a specified period of time, maybe 4 weeks. This could mean publishing in magazine, newspaper or other regularly scheduled publication.

You will then need to send proof of publication to the correct State office.

The next step is:

Applying for an EIN

In order for your nonprofit to get a bank account, apply for a credit card, apply for business permits or furnish independent contractors a Form 1099, you will need an Employer Identification Number (EIN).

An Employer Identification Number (EIN) is a nine-digit number assigned by the IRS. It is used to identify the tax accounts of employers and certain other organizations who do not have employees. It is a lot like a social security number for businesses.

Getting an EIN is really a very simple, yet crucial step, in the process of obtaining your 501(c)3 status. To obtain an EIN you will need to file Form SS-4 with the IRS. That form can be found at www.irs.gov. Make sure you download the most recent edition of that form.

The process to apply for an EIN is fast and easy. In most cases if you apply by phone you will receive your EIN immediately. Using the other methods are not as speedy. Still, the longest we have heard it taking to receive an EIN is 30 days.

You can apply in any of four ways. You can do it,

Online:

Go to www.irs.gov and type "How to apply for an EIN" in the search box.

FAX:

(859) 669-5760

Mail:

Internal Revenue Service

Attn: EIN Operation Cincinnati,

OH 45999

Telephone:

(267) 941-1099

The next step is:

Opening a Checking Account

Yep, you can do that now! It is a good idea to shop around to see which financial institution you want to do business with; different institutions have different fees and fees can add up.

Some banks are very supportive of nonprofits and a few will even help support your efforts with fundraising assistance. So, find the one that is best suited for what you are trying to accomplish.

Here is what the credit union or bank will need in order to open a checking account for your Organization:

1. A copy of your stamped Articles of Incorporation and Bylaws that shows that you filed with the appropriate State agency.

2. Board of Directors meeting minutes naming authorized signers.

The next step is:

Developing a Budget

When you apply to the Internal Revenue Service for consideration as a 501(c)3 Corporation under the Internal Revenue Code they will ask for a three year budget.

This can be a bit of a challenge, because at this point your Organization technically doesn't have any money.

Why does the Internal Revenue Service ask for this?

Basically, they want to see if you have thought this part of the plan through. And they want assurance that you are not using the designation merely as a way to avoid paying taxes.

There will be some serious red flags — and rightly so — if they see money coming in from you and then being paid to you for running the Organization. Building a budget for a nonprofit is very similar to building a budget for your business or for yourself. If you have Excel on your computer, it will be very helpful with this step.

Your budget needs to show where the income is coming from and how much. In this case an estimate. The budget will also need to show where the income is going.

Budget Breakdown

Use the following information as a guide to build your budget. Don't forget, the budget must account for three full years.

First Year

Income: The first year will obviously be the leanest, with most of the money coming from you, your Board members and maybe a couple of other people who believe in your Organization.

Expenses: Your first year's expenses will include the cost of forming your Organization. In fact, the cost of this book and our program can be one of those expenses. You will also have filing fees and possibly other expenses like hiring a graphic designer.

Even at this early stage you will want to show that a significant amount of the money your Organization received went towards the programs for which you are incorporating.

Second Year

Income: Here you will want to show that, along with money from you and your Board members, you plan to have a fundraiser or two.

Be reasonable with how much you think you can bring in from your fundraising efforts.

Expenses: Some of your expenses during the second year may be legal fees, bookkeeping fees, insurance, printing and postage costs, office supplies, some minimal equipment costs and event advertising costs for your fundraisers.

Your largest expense should be money you spend on the programs for which you incorporated as a nonprofit Organization.

Your goal is to have your expenses match your income.

Third Year

Income: By now the IRS is hoping that you are beginning to hit your stride with money coming in through Board donations, mail solicitations and fundraisers. At this point in your Organization's young life, it is not probable that you will be a recipient of a Grant.

Expenses:

Along with the expenses for years one and two, at this point you will undoubtedly
need to purchase additional office equipment and furniture.

You may even want to factor in the cost of office space and a small administrative expense.

The best rule of thumb this year is to work toward an 80/20 split of your resources, with 80 percent of the money received going toward programs and 20 percent going toward administration of the Organization

The last step in the process is:

Applying for Nonprofit Status

Yep, you read correctly. This is the final step. Here is what you have fulfilled to date that are all requirements in order to apply:

- You have established that your Organization exists for the public good.
- You have a Name.
- You have Articles of Incorporation & Bylaws.
- You have selected a Board of Directors.
- You have Incorporated.
- You have developed a three-year budget.

It is time to put it all together and apply for recognition as a 501(c)3 Corporation under the Internal Revenue Code. This will allow your Organization to receive tax exemption status.

Now, you must completely fill out the Form 1023 series application. This form can be located by going to www.irs.gov

As you fill out the application, the more detailed you can be, the less chance your application will be denied or that the Internal Revenue Service will ask for clarification.

Remember to:
- Fill the form out completely.
- Sign and date the form.
- Add the stated filing fee.
- Put the form and filing fee together in a large manila envelope and mail to the address listed on the form.

You will receive a letter from the Internal Revenue Service when your application has been received. If they have any questions about your application, they will contact you for clarification.

You can expect the consideration for recognition for tax exemption to take 12–24 months. The Internal Revenue Service will notify you by mail as to whether you have been accepted or rejected.

But wait, let me remind you of great news! Remember, you don't have to wait for the IRS response to begin living a passionately generous life. You can begin living out your passion right now through a fiscal sponsorship.

Fiscal Sponsorship

Remember, the Internal Revenue Service allows for a Corporation that has already been designated as a 501(c)3 to serve as a fiscal sponsor for other organizations. We have a nonprofit corporation called, 12oz of Hope, who's reason for existence is to assist people like you live a passionately generous life while you wait for approval of your application to be recognized by the IRS as a nonprofit corporation.

See it as an umbrella under which you and your group can function. Your Organization can still accomplish everything you hope to achieve with a 501(c)3 designation, you can even operate under your own name.

Send an email today to info@12ozofhope.org and put 'Fiscal Sponsor' in the Subject line.

Another nonprofit started by someone just like you that is making a difference....

Hope for Kids International

For over 40 years, we have been committed to serving children living in impoverished environments around the world by establishing economic, spiritual, water, orphan, and feeding programs. In addition to these programs, we have been leading teams of volunteers on two-week international mission trips bringing life-saving provisions and the spirit of Jesus.

Our vision is healing and empowering destitute communities with hope and necessary care to raise a new generation of healthy individuals who can break the generational curse of extreme poverty. We strive to meet this vision by building our Four Pillars of Hope: Health, Dignity, Joy, and Love. We exemplify the spirit of Jesus to show that all children are worthy of a prosperous life and bright future.

To bring hope and necessary care to kids through dignity, health, joy, and love.H4KI strives to restore dignity to innocent children and families who are suffering through extreme poverty and disease. We are bringing relief to poverty-stricken villages by providing clean water, building medical and dental clinics, and establishing emergency medical funds. Our strategies are designed to help villagers become self-sufficient through life-saving programs.

Chapter 10
Woot! Woot!

Celebrate & Plan for the Future

Wow! You did it!

I hope that you really take time out to celebrate. Do you
realize what you have already accomplished? It is not easy to
do what you have done! You may be like me. My tendency is
to work hard, reach a goal and instead of stopping and
enjoying the moment, I immediately start looking at the next
mountain to climb. But it is ok (and important!) to stop and
savor the moment. Recognize the accomplishment. Relish in
the achievement.

I have a friend who has a very unique tattoo on her leg. It is
simply the letter 'M' with a dot over it in block letters. Very
few people in the world have this tattoo. Have you seen it? It
is an Ironman tattoo.

Do you know what you need to accomplish in order to get
this tattoo? You have to have successfully finished an Ironman
triathlon. An Ironman Triathlon consists of a 2.4 mile swim, a

112 mile bicycle ride and a marathon 26.22 mile run, raced in that order without a break.

She did that!
Even more impressive is all the work she had to do in order to be able to even compete! She had to train for countless hours. She had to swim mind-numbing numbers of laps. She had to run hundreds of miles of bone jarring miles. She had to cycle thousands of lonely miles in order to just be in a position to complete. She had to increase her strength by lifting weights. She had to alter her diet so that her body could function as efficiently as possible. She had to say no to staying out late with friends so that she could get a proper amount of rest.

Similarly, there are multitudes of people who have wanted to compete in an 'Ironman Triathlon' – yours truly is one of them – but never have. Why? I haven't been willing to do what is necessary to qualify as an entrant into the competition.

There are multitudes of people who have in their heart to start a nonprofit so that they can live passionately generous lives. But that is far as they have gotten! Why? They haven't been willing to do what is necessary to qualify as an entrant in the arena of nonprofits. And because they don't it, there dream lays dormant.

Literally thousands of other people begin the process of training for an Ironman Triathlon and never actually compete. They drop out before reaching their goal. They have good intentions. They get up and run. They swim. They bike. But they don't know what they are doing.

Here are just a few of the things they don't know:
- How many miles to run each day.
- How many miles to bike each day.
- How many miles to swim.
- Let along the correct way to run, bike and swim.
- They don't know what their weight lifting program should consist of. They don't know what their diet should consist of.
- They don't know what kind of equipment they should by.

Similarly, there are thousands who begin the process to start their own nonprofit each year and because they don't get the right advice, never finish the task. Your willingness to do something about that passion burning in your heart, along with your willingness to seek out expert help sets you apart from the crowd. More importantly, it puts you on the right track to be able to live a passionately generous life and to make a real difference in life!

Look how far you have come. You have
accomplished all of the following:

- Developed your Vision Statement
- Established your Mission Statement
- Chosen a Name
- Registered your Name
- Identified who is going to help you
- Established expectations for the Board
- Chosen the Board
- Developed your Articles of Incorporation (Charter)
- Developed the Bylaws
- Incorporated in your host State
- Publicized your Incorporation
- Obtained an Employer Identification Number
- Opened a Bank Account
- Built a 3 year Budget,
- Applied for recognition for nonprofit status by the
  Internal Revenue Service.

Can you imagine doing all of that by yourself? Me neither! As
you look at that list, there are so many things that you did not
even have a clue were necessary in forming a nonprofit - let
alone know how to do it
So now what?

Remember my friend who competed in an Ironman Triathlon? She had trained for months, getting up at 4 a.m. each morning to work out. She had disciplined herself and ate only foods that would benefit her. She had purchased the perfect equipment so that her efforts could be maximized. She did everything her coach told her to do. She did all that so that she could be in a position to compete.

I remember when she was notified that she had been accepted as a competitor in the Ironman Triathlon. She was ecstatic. She whooped. She danced. She called all her friends. She celebrated – by allowing herself another piece of fruit!

It was a huge moment. What if she had done all that and then when the day came and it was time to compete she slept in? What if she had just rolled over and dreamt about the notice she had received that she was now qualified to compete?

She would have just thrown away the opportunity that she had worked so diligently to attain. If she had done that, she would have never realized her dream of competing in an Ironman Triathlon let alone be one of the few who finished and as a result could get the Ironman tattoo.

You are now at that same spot. You have been diligent. You have been disciplined. You have worked tirelessly. You have said 'No!' to fun activities you were invited to participate in so that you could concentrate on training. Soon you will receive notice that you have qualified to 'compete' as a nonprofit organization.

You have a couple of choices. After you celebrate – which you have every right to do - you could roll over and get some more sleep and dream about how fantastic it is that you qualified.

Or you can jump out of bed and say, 'Let's do it!' Let's actually do what we have qualified to do!

Receiving notice that your group has been recognized as a nonprofit corporation under section 501(c)3 by the Internal Revenue Service is not the finish line, it is the Starting line! Now you can do what you have been longing to do.

As you compete, know that there are many things that you will need to continue to learn in order for your organization to accomplish its purpose. What we have done to this point is established a foundation upon which you can build and grow and make a difference.

I want you to succeed. I want you to accomplish what you have set out to do. My desire for you is that you will be able to live a passionately generous life via your nonprofit and make the difference that you long to make. I want you to fulfill your passion!

With that in mind, I want to point out some things that you will need to learn as you continue on this epic journey of living a passionately generous life through your nonprofit.

Among them:
- How to run a *Board Meeting*
- How to keep *Official Records* of your Board Meetings.
- How to *Brand* your Organization.
- How to create a *Fundraising Campaign*
- How to *Apply for Grants*
- How to use *Social Media* to raise awareness and money
- How and when to add *Staff* to your Organization
- How to create a *Business Plan*
- And more.

Please don't try to do it alone. Find resources to help you. Seek out and listen to expert help.

Another nonprofit started by someone just like you that is making a difference…

Trevor's Vision

The group is affectionately named "Trevor's Vision" after the little boy in the movie 'Pay it Forward'. His vision was to simply do a few random acts of kindness and in turn maybe inspire a few people to do the same which could potentially change the world. That is exactly what we feel like we are doing, Changing the world one person at a time.

Jeff Kistler, along with another friend, were inspired to help feed the homeless about 10 years ago when we saw a story on the local news, Channel 5, honoring a family who was feeding the homeless in Margret T Hance Park. We came down to meet the family and immediately got involved. When that family fell on hard times we picked up the ball and ran with it. I enlisted the help of some great friends who have the same vision of giving back that I do.

We started with the last Thursday of the month and through generous donations have grown our little charity to feed EVERY Thursday night and are in the process of adding a second night.

I am very encouraged and proud of the work we have done so far. The last three years we have been able to put a new pair of shoes and socks on each homeless person at Christmas time (about 200 pairs of shoes each year). We have given each person hygiene kits, blankets, jackets, sweatshirts, sleeping bags along with a weekly hot meal and fellowship.
This whole experience has been very eye opening for me. Not only have I learned that most people are good-natured and

truly want to help others, but how genuinely good it makes us feel when we do it. God has truly wired us to love our neighbors. I have also learned that you "can't out-give God". Every time we set these lofty goals of purchasing 200 pairs of shoes or growing this homeless ministry to add another week, He meets us right where we are at and helps us accomplish those goals, all in His name. We truly thank you for the opportunity to serve and look forward too many more years to come. I'm excited to see what God has in store for our future.

Chapter 11
With Your Success in Mind

Let us help you!

It has been a pleasure to walk you through these steps. I find my fulfillment in helping others help others!

If at any point in this process you get tripped up, reach out to us at info@espressofornoprofits.com. We have a service where we can walk you through this process from A-Z.

If you did follow the steps in this book and are now recognized as a 501(c)3 corporation by the Internal Revenue Service you have established your nonprofit on a strong foundation upon which to build. I want to help you as you continue leading your nonprofit. There are a lot of obstacles that can trip you up – with my help we can get through them so that your organization has a strong future fulfilling its purpose.

Send us an email at info@giveservelive.com and say "Help me!"

There are a lot of challenges you will face. Yes, you have already accomplished a huge task by officially making application to be recognized as a nonprofit corporation under Section 501(c)3 of the Internal Revenue Service.

Not long ago the founder of a nonprofit called me and asked for my assistance. They were in a real mess. So much so that they were in jeopardy of losing their nonprofit status.

I had originally helped them start their organization and that is why they knew they could turn to me. After meeting with their board and reviewing the minutes of their Board meetings, I presented to them the steps necessary to rectify their dilemma.

While their intentions were great, they hadn't followed the procedure that they had promised to adhere to in their Articles and Bylaws. We rolled up our sleeves and, over a period of time, got them back on track.

I love to help organizations stay on track and to grow. The only thing worse than not starting your own nonprofit is starting it and then having to close it down because of an oversight.

You will continue to need expert advice. Do you know how to set up a Capital Campaign? Do you know the importance of branding? Do you know how to run a Board Meeting? Do you know how to keep records of your Board Meetings? Do you know how to file your annual report to the IRS? Do you know how to make changes to your Bylaws?

In our 'Do It Yourself' culture we fail to recognize that sometimes we need an expert. Yes, there are many things you can teach yourself how to do.

You can probably learn how to unstop your own drains. You can maybe learn how to fix your dishwasher. You can even figure out how to replace your roof. You may learn how to replace the engine of your motorcycle. However, in each of these you will undoubtedly look to a source of information to learn how to do it.

You might go to the hardware store and ask the associate how to unclog a drain. You may watch YouTube to learn how to repair your dishwasher or repair your roof. You may buy a manual to walk you through each step of repairing your motorcycle.

But notice each time you looked to some who had done it before to teach you how to do it.

There are some things that even the most avid 'Do It Yourselfer' can't do. For example, if your friend has a heart attack you don't run to the store and look for a manual on how to fix his heart. You don't search YouTube to figure out how to perform bypass surgery.

No! You dial 911 – and you do it as quickly as possible – so that your friend can get expert advice and survive.

When your nonprofit needs help – and believe me, it will! Let us help! See us as the people who answers your 911call.

Don't jeopardize your organization's future by not running a Board meeting correctly.

Don't jeopardize your opportunity to make a difference by not keeping legal records.

Don't jeopardize the opportunity to put your best foot forward by overlooking the importance of Branding.

Don't jeopardize your organization's existence ignoring your mistake and hoping the IRS will go away.

Let us help!